AUSTRALIA TRAV

Discover Australia 2024

By

Nancy A. Morrison

TABLE OF CONTENT

Chapter 3. Must-Visit Destinations

3.1 Sydney

3.2 Great Barrier Reef

3.3 The Outback

Chapter 4. Activities and Attractions

4.1 Wildlife encounters

4.2 Outdoor adventures

Chapter 5.Cultural experiences

5.1 Food and Drink

5.2 Australian cuisine

5.3 Dining etiquette

Chapter 1. Introduction

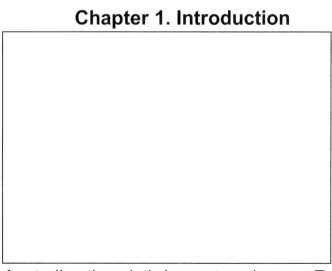

Australia, the sixth-largest nation on Earth, is a continent encircled by the Pacific and Indian Oceans. This island nation has always captivated the interest of tourists and explorers due to its distinctive animals, varied landscapes, and energetic cities. It has been doing so for generations.

Aboriginal Australians, the indigenous inhabitants, have a rich cultural history spanning over 65,000 years. Their deep connection to the land is evident in intricate Dreamtime stories, which explain the creation of the world and its features. The iconic Uluru, a massive sandstone monolith, stands as a sacred symbol of this ancient heritage.

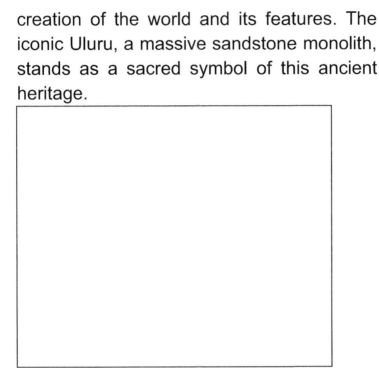

Australia's colonization by Europeans began in 1788 when Captain James Cook claimed the eastern coast for Britain. This marked the start of a tumultuous history, including the forced relocation and mistreatment of indigenous peoples. Today, efforts are ongoing to reconcile and address the historical injustices suffered by Aboriginal communities.

The country's geography is as diverse as its history. The vast Outback, an arid interior, contrasts sharply with the lush rainforests of Queensland and the pristine beaches that stretch along the coastline. The Great Barrier Reef, the world's largest coral reef system, is a UNESCO World Heritage Site and a testament to Australia's ecological significance.

Australia's wildlife is equally unique. Kangaroos, koalas, and wombats are just a few of the marsupials that call the country home. The continent's isolation has led to the evolution of distinct flora and fauna, making Australia a haven for nature enthusiasts and researchers alike.

In terms of governance, Australia operates as a federal parliamentary constitutional monarchy. The Queen of England serves as the monarch, represented locally by the Governor-General. The political landscape is dominated by two major parties, the Australian Labor Party and the Liberal Party, reflecting a stable democratic system.

Economically, Australia has thrived on its rich natural resources, including coal, iron ore, and gold. The service sector, particularly finance and tourism, also plays a significant role. Sydney, with its iconic

Opera House and Harbour Bridge, is a global financial hub, while Melbourne is renowned for its cultural diversity and vibrant arts scene.

Sport is a national passion in Australia. Cricket, rugby, and Australian rules football command widespread attention, fostering a sense of camaraderie among citizens. The country's sporting achievements, both nationally and internationally, contribute to a strong sense of national identity.

The Australian lifestyle is often characterized by a laid-back attitude, known colloquially as the "Aussie way of life." This is reflected in the outdoor activities that Australians cherish, from surfing on Bondi Beach to hiking in the Blue Mountains. Barbecues, known as "barbies," are a social institution, that brings friends and families together.

Education is a priority, with a high standard of schools and universities attracting students from around the world. The University of Sydney and the Australian National University are renowned for their academic excellence, contributing to Australia's reputation as a global education destination.

Despite its many strengths, Australia faces challenges such as climate change, environmental conservation, and issues related to the rights and well-being of indigenous populations. Ongoing efforts are being made to address these concerns and ensure a sustainable and inclusive future for all Australians.

In conclusion, Australia's allure lies in its rich cultural tapestry, diverse landscapes, and resilient spirit that has overcome challenges throughout history. From the ancient stories of the Dreamtime to the bustling cities of today, Australia continues to captivate the world with its unique blend of tradition, innovation, and natural beauty.

1.1 Geography and Climate

The sixth-largest country in the world, Australia, is renowned for its distinctive topography and varied climate. Positioned between the Pacific and Indian Oceans, the continent country covers an area of roughly 7.7 million square kilometers. Its diverse geographic features, which span from lush rainforests to arid deserts, contribute to a wide range of temperatures and ecosystems

The Great Dividing Range, one of Australia's prominent geographical features, runs parallel to the east coast. This mountain range influences the climate on either side, creating distinct differences between the eastern and western regions. The eastern coastal areas experience a temperate climate, characterized by moderate temperatures and well-distributed rainfall. Sydney and Brisbane, major cities along the east coast, benefit from this climate, fostering diverse flora and fauna.

Conversely, the western part of Australia is marked by vast arid and semi-arid regions, including the iconic Outback. The Outback, characterized by its red, sandy terrain, showcases the aridity of the continent. With limited rainfall, the flora and fauna in these regions have adapted to survive in harsh conditions. Iconic species like kangaroos and emus are well-suited to the arid landscapes of central Australia.

Australia's interior is dominated by deserts, notably the Simpson Desert, Gibson Desert, and Great Victoria Desert. These arid expanses experience scorching temperatures during the day and can be surprisingly cold at night. The famous Uluru, a massive sandstone monolith, is situated in the heart of the continent, symbolizing the stark beauty of the Australian Outback.

Moving towards the north, tropical climates prevail in areas like northern Queensland and the Northern Territory. The tropical north experiences distinct wet and dry seasons, influenced by the Australian monsoon. During the wet season, heavy rainfall is common, leading to lush vegetation and vibrant ecosystems. The Great Barrier Reef, the world's largest coral reef system, lies off the northeast coast, contributing to the region's ecological richness.

Australia's southern regions, including Victoria, Tasmania, and parts of South Australia, feature a cooler climate, with four distinct seasons. Melbourne, for instance, is known for its variable weather, ranging from hot summers to chilly winters. The diversity in climate across the continent allows for a broad range of agricultural activities, from wine production in cooler regions to extensive cattle farming in the arid interior.

Australia's island state, Tasmania, showcases a unique blend of temperate rainforests, alpine landscapes, and pristine coastlines. Its cooler climate supports a variety of flora and fauna, some of which are not found on the mainland. Cradle Mountain-Lake St Clair National Park exemplifies Tasmania's natural beauty, offering opportunities for hiking and wildlife observation.

In terms of human settlement, major cities like Sydney, Melbourne, Brisbane, Perth, and Adelaide are located along the coast, benefiting from access to water resources and milder climates. These urban centers contribute significantly to Australia's economic and cultural landscape.

In conclusion, Australia's geography and climate are incredibly diverse, ranging from the arid Outback to the tropical rainforests and temperate coastal regions. This diversity not only shapes the physical characteristics of the continent but also influences the lifestyles and activities of its inhabitants. From the iconic landmarks of the Outback to the vibrant ecosystems of the Great Barrier Reef, Australia stands as a testament to the marvels of nature and the adaptability of life in various environments.

1.2 Customs and festival events

Australia is a multicultural country, and this rich tapestry is reflected in its festivals and customs. The nation has an exciting calendar full of activities that unite communities, from multicultural celebrations to indigenous rituals.

One of the most significant events on the Australian calendar is Australia Day, celebrated on January 26th. It marks the anniversary of the arrival of the First Fleet in 1788 and is a day for Australians to come together and reflect on their national identity. Festivities include citizenship ceremonies, barbecues, and fireworks, with many people proudly displaying the Australian flag.

Indigenous Australians also have their unique customs and celebrations. NAIDOC Week, held in July, is a time to honor the history, culture, and achievements of Aboriginal and Torres Strait Islander peoples. Traditional dances, art exhibitions, and cultural performances are integral parts of these celebrations, providing a platform for Indigenous voices to be heard.

Easter is another major festival in Australia, observed with a blend of religious and secular traditions. Many Australians participate in the Easter Bilby campaign, raising awareness about endangered native species. Easter egg hunts, church services, and family gatherings are common during this time.

As the winter chill sets in, Australians gear up for the Winter Festival in cities like Sydney and Melbourne. Ice skating rinks, winter markets, and light displays transform urban spaces into winter wonderlands, offering a unique experience in a country known for its warm climate.

Harmony Day, celebrated on March 21st, promotes inclusivity and cultural diversity.

Australians of all backgrounds come together to share their traditions through music, dance, and food. The message is one of unity and respect, emphasizing the importance of cultural acceptance.

In November, Australians commemorate Remembrance Day to honor the sacrifices of those who served in the armed forces. A minute of silence is observed at 11 am, and red poppies are worn as a symbol of remembrance. This day provides an opportunity for reflection and gratitude for the contributions of the military.

The Melbourne Cup, known as "the race that stops a nation," is a horse racing event held on the first Tuesday of November. While it's a major sporting event, it's also a day when workplaces pause, and people gather to watch the race. Fashion and socializing are key elements of this iconic event.

Multiculturalism is a cornerstone of Australian society, and this is celebrated during the various cultural festivals throughout the year. The Chinese New Year festivities, Diwali, and the Greek Glendi Festival are just a few examples of events where communities share their cultural heritage with the wider population.

Christmas in Australia is a unique experience due to its occurrence during the Southern Hemisphere's summer. While the cultural elements of gift-giving and feasting remain, Australians often celebrate with barbecues, beach outings, and outdoor activities. Carols by Candlelight events are held nationwide, bringing communities together in a festive spirit.

In addition to these nationally recognized festivals, each state and territory in Australia has its local events and traditions. For instance, the Sydney Festival in January showcases a diverse range of artistic performances, while the Royal Queensland Show, known as the Ekka, is a major agricultural show in Brisbane.

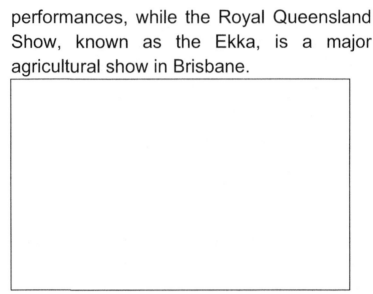

In conclusion, Australia's customs and festival activities are a reflection of its diverse society. From indigenous celebrations to multicultural festivals, each event contributes to the unique tapestry of Australian culture, fostering a sense of unity and pride among its people.

Chapter 2.Planning Your Trip

2.1 Language and Communication

With a history deeply rooted in Indigenous cultures and a contemporary landscape shaped by waves of immigration, the linguistic landscape of Australia is as varied as its geographical features.

At the heart of Australia's linguistic diversity is the enduring presence of Indigenous languages, spoken by the Aboriginal and Torres Strait Islander peoples. These languages, characterized by their unique phonetic structures and rich oral traditions, have been crucial in preserving and passing down cultural heritage. However, the impact of colonization has led to the decline of many Indigenous languages, highlighting the ongoing efforts to revitalize and preserve this vital aspect of Australia's linguistic heritage.

English, introduced by British settlers in the late 18th century, has become the dominant language in Australia. However, Australian English has developed its distinct features, including colloquialisms, accent variations, and a unique vocabulary that reflects the nation's cultural identity. The use of slang, such as "mate" and "g'day," is ingrained in everyday communication, fostering a sense of camaraderie and informality.

Beyond English, Australia hosts a mosaic of languages reflecting its multicultural society. Migration waves from Europe, Asia, and the Middle East have contributed to a linguistic kaleidoscope, with communities maintaining their native languages while embracing

English as a common means of communication. For instance, Italian, Greek, Mandarin, Arabic, and Punjabi are among the many languages spoken in Australian households, creating a vibrant linguistic landscape.

In urban centers like Sydney and Melbourne, the multicultural nature of the population is evident in the diversity of languages heard on the streets. This linguistic richness is not confined to private spaces; it permeates public life, with multilingual signs, cultural festivals, and community events celebrating the multitude of languages spoken across the country.

Education plays a pivotal role in shaping language use in Australia. English is the primary medium of instruction in schools, but efforts are made to incorporate the teaching of Indigenous languages and the inclusion of multicultural perspectives in the curriculum. Language programs and initiatives aim to promote linguistic diversity, fostering an appreciation for different languages and cultures among the younger generation.

In the realm of digital communication, the internet and social media have further transformed the way Australians communicate. The digital age has facilitated the exchange of ideas and information across linguistic and cultural boundaries, connecting people from diverse backgrounds. Social media platforms, in particular, have become spaces where individuals express themselves in a myriad of languages, contributing to a virtual representation of Australia's linguistic diversity.

Despite these positive aspects, challenges exist in ensuring linguistic inclusivity. Language proficiency, especially in English, can impact access to education, employment, and social opportunities.

Efforts are underway to address language barriers through language support programs and initiatives that promote language learning and inclusion.

Australia's linguistic landscape is a dynamic reflection of its rich cultural tapestry. From the enduring languages of its Indigenous peoples to the myriad languages spoken by its diverse population, Australia embraces a linguistic diversity that is both a source of strength and a challenge to navigate. In a globalized world, the ability to communicate across languages is an asset, and Australia's commitment to preserving its linguistic heritage while embracing new linguistic influences positions it as a vibrant and inclusive society on the global stage.

2.2 Visa requirements

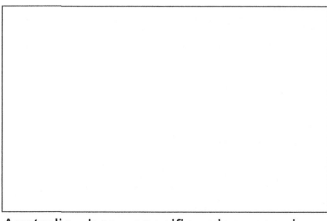

Australia has specific visa requirements depending on the purpose of your visit. The following is a detailed overview of various visa categories, their requirements, and the application process.

1. Visitor Visas

Tourist Stream (subclass 600): This visa is for people coming to Australia for a holiday, to visit family and friends, or for other short-term non-work purposes. Requirements include proof of funds, health insurance, and a genuine intention to stay temporarily.

Electronic Travel Authority (subclass 601)

Available for passport holders from certain countries, this visa allows short visits for tourism or business purposes. It's applied online and is linked to the passport electronically.

2. Work Visas

Temporary Skill Shortage (subclass 482): For skilled workers nominated by an approved employer to fill labor shortages. Requires sponsorship from an eligible employer, relevant skills assessment, and health insurance.

Skilled Independent Visa (subclass 189): Points-based visa for skilled workers without the need for employer sponsorship. Applicants must meet the points threshold based on factors like age, English proficiency, and work experience.

3. Family Visas

Partner Visas (subclass 820/801): For those married to or in a de facto relationship with an Australian citizen, permanent resident, or eligible New Zealand citizen. Proof of relationship, health, and character assessments are required.

Parent Visas (subclass 103): For parents of Australian citizens or permanent residents. Requires sponsorship from a child, assurance of support, and a balance-of-family test.

4. Student Visas

Student Visa (subclass 500): For international students enrolled in a registered course of study. Requires an acceptance letter from an Australian educational institution, proof of financial capacity, and health insurance.

5. Business and Investment Visas

Business Innovation and Investment Visa (subclass 188): For individuals with business or investment skills who want to establish, develop, or manage a business in Australia. Requires nomination by a state or territory government.

Investor Visa (subclass 891): For individuals who have maintained an investment in Australia for four years. Applicants must meet specific financial and business criteria.

6. Refugee and Humanitarian Visas

Refugee and Humanitarian Program: Australia offers protection for refugees and those in humanitarian need. Applications are usually made offshore, and eligibility criteria depend

2.3 Best time to visit

The best time to visit depends on your preferences, interests, and the specific regions you plan to explore.

Summer (December to February)

This is the peak tourist season in Australia, especially in the southern parts like Sydney and Melbourne. The weather is hot and dry, making it ideal for beach activities, outdoor events, and exploring iconic landmarks. However, popular destinations can be crowded, and prices for accommodation and tours may be higher.

Autumn (March to May)

Autumn brings milder temperatures and less crowded attractions. It's a great time to visit the southern regions as the weather is still pleasant, and the landscapes are often adorned with colorful foliage. Autumn is also a good time to explore the wine regions,

such as the Barossa Valley in South
Australia.

Winter (June to August)

Winter varies across Australia. In the
northern parts (Queensland, Northern
Territory), it's dry and warm, making it a
suitable time for exploring the Great Barrier
Reef or visiting the Outback. In the southern
regions, it can get chilly, and snowfall is
possible in the alpine areas, providing
opportunities for skiing and winter sports.

Spring (September to November)

Spring is a delightful time to visit as
temperatures start to rise, and flowers
bloom. It's an excellent season for outdoor
activities, including hiking and wildlife
watching. The Great Ocean Road in Victoria
and the Blue Mountains in New South
Wales are particularly beautiful during
spring.

Considerations

Events and Festivals: Check the local events and festivals happening during your visit. Australia hosts various cultural, sports, and music events throughout the year.

Wildlife Watching: If you're interested in wildlife, different seasons offer unique opportunities. For example, winter is the prime whale-watching season along the East Coast.

Northern vs. Southern Hemisphere

Remember that Australia is in the southern hemisphere, so seasons are opposite to those in the northern hemisphere.

Budget and Crowds: Travel costs and crowds can vary by season. Booking in advance and traveling during shoulder seasons can help you save money and avoid peak crowds.

Ultimately, the best time to visit Australia depends on your preferences and the experiences you're seeking. Whether you're a beach lover, an adventure seeker, or a culture enthusiast, there's a season that suits your interests in the Land Down Under.

2.4.Budgeting and currency

Creating a budget for a trip to Australia involves careful planning and consideration of various expenses. Australia is known for its diverse landscapes, unique wildlife, and vibrant cities, making it a popular destination. To ensure a smooth and enjoyable trip, it's crucial to budget for accommodation, transportation, food, activities, and account for currency exchange rates.

Accommodation

Start by researching accommodation options. Australia offers a range of choices, from budget hostels to luxury hotels. Consider the duration of your stay and the cities or regions you plan to visit. Booking in advance can often secure better rates. Additionally, explore alternative accommodation options such as Airbnb or vacation rentals for potential cost savings.

Transportation

Australia is vast, and getting around requires careful planning. If you're covering long distances, consider domestic flights, but book early for better deals. For shorter distances, public transportation, rental cars, or even camper vans are viable options. Research transportation passes or discount cards that might offer savings on buses, trains, or ferries.

Food

Food expenses can vary, so plan accordingly. Eating out in restaurants can be pricey, but you can save money by exploring local markets or opting for takeaway options. Consider a mix of dining experiences to balance your budget. Also, factor in occasional splurges on unique local cuisine.

Activities

Australia offers a plethora of activities, ranging from guided tours to outdoor adventures. Research attractions and activities in advance to estimate costs. Some natural wonders and national parks may have entry fees. Look for bundled deals or passes that offer discounts on multiple attractions.

Currency Exchange

Understand the currency exchange rates and fees associated with converting your money to Australian dollars. Utilize reliable currency converters or financial apps to stay updated on the latest rates. Consider exchanging some currency before your trip, but be cautious with large amounts due to security concerns.

Budgeting Tips

Emergency Fund: Set aside a portion of your budget as an emergency fund for unexpected expenses.

Contingency Planning: Plan for unforeseen circumstances, such as flight delays or medical emergencies, by having travel insurance.

Local SIM Card: If you plan to use your phone in Australia, consider getting a local SIM card to avoid high roaming charges.

Currency for Australia

The official currency of Australia is the Australian Dollar (AUD). Check for the latest exchange rates before exchanging your money. While credit cards are widely accepted, it's advisable to carry some cash for smaller transactions, especially in remote areas.

In conclusion, careful budgeting is essential for a successful trip to Australia. By planning and considering all potential expenses, you can make the most of your journey without overspending. Keep flexibility in your budget for unexpected opportunities or expenses, ensuring a memorable and stress-free travel experience.

2.5 Accommodation Option

Hotels and Resorts

Australia boasts a plethora of hotels and resorts, ranging from budget to luxury. Cities like Sydney, Melbourne, and Brisbane feature renowned international chains, while coastal areas offer resorts with stunning views.

Serviced Apartments

Ideal for extended stays, serviced apartments provide a home-like environment with kitchen facilities and housekeeping services. Major cities offer a variety of options, giving guests flexibility and convenience.

Hostels

Popular among budget travelers, hostels are scattered across Australia, especially in urban areas and tourist destinations. They offer shared dormitories or private rooms, fostering a social atmosphere for backpackers.

Guesthouses and Bed & Breakfasts

Charming guesthouses and B&Bs are prevalent in smaller towns and rural areas. They offer a more personalized experience, often with local hosts providing insights into the region's culture.

Holiday Parks

Caravan parks and holiday parks are prevalent in coastal and scenic areas. They provide a range of accommodation, from campsites to cabins, and often include recreational facilities like swimming pools and barbecue areas.

Airbnb and Vacation Rentals

Airbnb has gained popularity in Australia, offering a variety of accommodations such as apartments, houses, and unique stays. This option is prevalent in both urban and rural settings.

Farm Stays

For a unique experience, consider a farm stay. This option allows guests to immerse themselves in rural life, participating in farm activities while enjoying comfortable accommodations.

Camping

Australia's vast landscapes make it a camping paradise. National parks and designated camping areas provide opportunities to experience the great outdoors. Be sure to adhere to camping regulations and respect the environment.

Luxury Lodges

For those seeking opulence, Australia offers luxury lodges in stunning natural settings. These lodges often provide exclusive experiences, gourmet dining, and spa facilities.

Backpacker Motels

Catering to budget-conscious travelers, backpacker motels offer simple and affordable accommodations. These can be found in both cities and smaller towns.

University Accommodation

In major cities with universities, you may find accommodation options on campus during academic breaks. This can be network

2.6 Transportation

Australia, a vast continent surrounded by the Indian and Pacific Oceans, offers a diverse range of transportation options to explore its unique landscapes and vibrant cities. Whether you're a traveler seeking adventure or a business professional attending meetings, Australia provides various modes of transportation to suit your needs.

Air Travel

The most common and efficient way to reach Australia from international destinations is by air. Major cities like Sydney, Melbourne, Brisbane, and Perth have international airports with well-connected routes. International airlines operate regular flights to these cities, ensuring convenient access for travelers from around the globe.

Domestically, Australia boasts an extensive network of airports, facilitating quick and comfortable air travel between cities and regional areas. Airlines such as Qantas,

Virgin Australia, and Jetstar dominate the domestic market, offering frequent flights and competitive pricing.

Rail Travel

For those seeking a scenic journey, Australia's rail network provides a unique way to traverse the continent. The iconic Indian Pacific connects Sydney on the east coast to Perth on the west, covering a staggering distance of over 4,000 kilometers. The Ghan travels north-south, linking Adelaide to Darwin, crossing the captivating landscapes of the Outback.

In addition to these transcontinental services, various other train routes crisscross the country, offering a comfortable and leisurely mode of transportation. The Great Southern Railways, which operates these iconic trains, ensures passengers experience the diverse beauty of Australia's interior.

Road Trips

Australia's well-maintained road infrastructure encourages road trips, allowing travelers to explore the country at their own pace. Rental cars are readily available at airports and major cities, providing the flexibility to create personalized itineraries. The Great Ocean Road in Victoria, stretching along the stunning coastline, is a popular choice for road trippers, offering breathtaking views and iconic landmarks like the Twelve Apostles.

Greyhound Australia, a long-distance bus service, connects cities and regional centers, providing an affordable and convenient option for those who prefer not to drive. Intercity coaches are equipped with modern amenities, making the journey comfortable and enjoyable.

Public Transport

Australia's major cities have efficient public transportation systems, including buses, trains, and trams. In cities like Sydney and Melbourne, extensive networks of trains and trams cover both the central business districts and surrounding suburbs. Public buses complement these services, providing a comprehensive transit experience.

Chapter 3. Must-Visit Destinations

3.1 Sydney

Sydney, Australia, a vibrant metropolis, captivates visitors with its iconic landmarks, diverse culture, and stunning landscapes. Nestled on the east coast, Sydney is the capital of New South Wales and stands as one of the country's most populous and influential cities.

The Sydney Opera House, an architectural masterpiece, graces the harbor, symbolizing the city's global identity. Its distinctive sail-like shells attract millions of tourists annually, offering a venue for world-class performances. Adjacent to the Opera House, the Sydney Harbour Bridge spans the waters, providing a breathtaking view of the city skyline and the harbor below.

As the sun sets, the city comes alive with the illuminated skyline reflecting in the harbor. Circular Quay, a bustling waterfront precinct, becomes a hub of activity, with ferries departing for various destinations, street performers captivating audiences, and diners enjoying waterfront restaurants.

Sydney's beaches are legendary, with Bondi Beach standing out as a global icon. The golden sands stretch along the coastline, inviting surfers, sunbathers, and beach enthusiasts. Bondi's laid-back atmosphere contrasts with the energetic vibe of Manly

Beach, accessible by a scenic ferry ride, offering a different coastal experience.

In the heart of the city, Hyde Park provides a green oasis for relaxation and recreation. Surrounded by historic landmarks, including the ANZAC War Memorial, the park is a peaceful retreat from the urban hustle. Nearby, the Royal Botanic Garden showcases a diverse collection of plant species and offers a serene escape with views of the Sydney skyline.

Sydney's cultural diversity is evident in neighborhoods like Chinatown, where bustling markets and authentic eateries transport visitors to the heart of Asia. The Rocks, with its cobblestone streets and historic buildings, preserves the city's colonial past, while vibrant street markets add a contemporary flair.

The city's culinary scene is a fusion of global influences, with trendy cafes, fine dining restaurants, and multicultural eateries lining the streets. From seafood at the Sydney Fish Market to gourmet experiences in Surry Hills, Sydney satisfies every palate.

Sport holds a special place in Sydney's heart, with iconic venues like the Sydney Cricket Ground hosting major events. The city's passion for sports extends to the annual Sydney New Year's Eve fireworks, a spectacular display that lights up the harbor and draws spectators from around the world.

Sydney's public transport system, including trains, buses, and ferries, efficiently connects its diverse neighborhoods. The efficient infrastructure complements the city's commitment to sustainability, reflected in initiatives like the Green Square urban renewal project.

Beyond the urban landscape, the Blue Mountains offer a natural retreat just a short drive from the city. Scenic lookouts, hiking trails, and the iconic Three Sisters rock formation showcase the region's natural beauty. Meanwhile, the Hunter Valley, a renowned wine-producing area, invites visitors to indulge in vineyard tours and tastings.

Sydney, with its dynamic blend of nature and culture, modernity and tradition, stands as a testament to Australia's allure. Whether exploring iconic landmarks, savoring diverse cuisines, or unwinding on golden beaches, Sydney invites travelers to experience a city that seamlessly blends sophistication with a laid-back charm.

3.2 Great Barrier Reef

The Great Barrier Reef, located off the coast of Queensland, Australia, is the largest coral reef system on the planet, spanning over 2,300 kilometers. This natural wonder is not just a collection of vibrant corals; it's a complex ecosystem that supports an incredible diversity of marine life. Comprising thousands of individual reefs and islands, the Great Barrier Reef is a UNESCO World Heritage Site, recognized for its ecological significance.

The reef's intricate beauty lies in its corals, which are colonies of tiny animals called polyps. These polyps secrete calcium carbonate, forming the stunning structures that make up the reef. The colors of the corals are a result of a symbiotic relationship with algae living within their tissues, providing them with nutrients and vibrant hues.

Beyond its aesthetic allure, the Great Barrier Reef serves as a critical habitat for an astonishing array of marine species. From the charismatic clownfish to the majestic humpback whales, the reef supports an estimated 1,500 species of fish, 400 types of coral, and a multitude of other organisms, many of which are not found anywhere else on Earth.

However, the reef faces numerous threats, primarily from climate change. Rising sea temperatures due to global warming result in coral bleaching, a phenomenon where corals expel their colorful algae, leaving them vulnerable to disease and death. Additionally, ocean acidification, caused by the absorption of excess carbon dioxide, poses a threat to the ability of corals to build their skeletons.

Human activities, such as overfishing and pollution, further compound the challenges facing the Great Barrier Reef. Efforts are underway to mitigate these impacts through conservation initiatives, including marine protected areas and sustainable tourism practices. The Australian government, in collaboration with scientists and environmental organizations, is actively involved in safeguarding this natural wonder.

Tourism plays a significant role in the region's economy, attracting millions of visitors each year who come to witness the reef's unparalleled beauty. However, striking a balance between tourism and conservation is crucial to ensure the long-term survival of the Great Barrier Reef. Sustainable practices, such as reef-friendly sunscreen use and responsible boating, are essential to minimize human impact.

Research and monitoring programs continuously strive to understand the reef's dynamics and identify strategies for its preservation. Scientists exploring innovative techniques, including coral breeding programs and the development of heat-resistant corals, to enhance the reef's resilience in the face of climate change.

In conclusion, the Great Barrier Reef stands as a testament to the breathtaking diversity of marine life on our planet. Its intricate ecosystems are a source of wonder and inspiration, but they are also fragile and facing unprecedented challenges. The collective efforts of governments, scientists, and the public are crucial to ensuring the preservation of this natural marvel for generations to come.

3.3 The Outback

The Australian Outback is an expansive and rugged landscape, characterized by vast deserts, red-earth plains, and iconic landmarks such as Uluru. Its harsh conditions create a unique environment where survival requires adaptation and resilience. The region's flora and fauna have evolved to thrive in this arid setting, showcasing a remarkable array of native species.

The Outback's rich indigenous history is deeply intertwined with the land, as Aboriginal communities have maintained a spiritual connection for thousands of years. Dreamtime stories pass down cultural knowledge, emphasizing the significance of the landscape and its role in sustaining life.

Beyond the natural beauty, the Outback is a haven for adventure seekers. The legendary Birdsville Track and the rugged Gibb River Road attract intrepid travelers, offering a taste of the vastness and isolation that defines the region. The remote opal-mining town of Coober Pedy, where homes are built underground to escape the scorching temperatures, reflects the resourcefulness required to thrive in this unforgiving environment.

Stargazing in the Outback is a breathtaking experience, with the lack of light pollution revealing a celestial spectacle. The night sky becomes a canvas painted with constellations, emphasizing the isolation and tranquility of this remote expanse.

Despite its challenges, the Outback has played a crucial role in shaping the Australian identity. The resilience of the people who call it home, along with the stories of exploration and survival, contribute to a narrative of endurance and tenacity. The vastness of the Outback reminds us of the sheer magnitude of our planet and the beauty found in the most unexpected places.

Chapter 4. Activities and Attractions

4.1 Wildlife encounters

Australia is a continent teeming with unique and diverse wildlife, offering encounters that captivate the imagination. From the iconic kangaroos and koalas to the more elusive creatures, the Australian landscape is a haven for nature enthusiasts seeking unforgettable wildlife experiences

In the lush rainforests of Queensland, the vibrant and elusive cassowary roams. This large flightless bird, with its striking blue and black plumage, is considered a keystone species in the region. Encountering a cassowary in the wild is a rare and awe-inspiring event, as these creatures navigate the dense foliage with surprising agility. Their presence underscores the delicate balance of the rainforest ecosystem they call home.

Venturing into the arid interior, one may cross paths with the iconic kangaroo, bounding gracefully across the vast plains. These marsupials, with their distinctive hopping gait, are a symbol of Australia's unique fauna. Observing a kangaroo in its natural habitat provides a glimpse into the adaptability required to survive in harsh outback conditions.

The coastal waters offer a different realm of wildlife encounters, with the majestic humpback whales undertaking their annual migration along the east and west coasts.

Witnessing these colossal marine mammals breaching and tail-slapping is a humbling experience, highlighting the importance of Australia's marine environments as crucial habitats for these gentle giants.

Australia's oceans are also home to the awe-inspiring Great Barrier Reef, a UNESCO World Heritage site, and the world's largest coral reef system. Snorkeling or diving in these crystal-clear waters opens a portal to an underwater wonderland, where technicolor coral formations provide a backdrop for an astonishing array of marine life, from graceful sea turtles to the vibrant clownfish darting among the anemones.

For those seeking a more intimate encounter, the koala sanctuaries scattered across the country offer a chance to observe these iconic marsupials up close. Nestled in the branches of eucalyptus trees, koalas epitomize the charm of Australia's wildlife. Visitors can learn about conservation efforts and gain insight into the unique dietary habits and behaviors that define these cuddly creatures.

Australia's avian diversity is equally captivating, with the flamboyant lorikeets and the iconic kookaburra contributing to the symphony of bird calls in the early morning. The elusive lyrebird, known for its remarkable ability to mimic natural and artificial sounds, adds an enchanting element to the forest soundtrack.

In the heart of the Red Centre, the enigmatic thorny devil, a master of camouflage, blends seamlessly with the arid landscape. This unique lizard, adorned with spines and a distinctive pattern, exemplifies the adaptations necessary for survival in the harsh desert environment. Encountering a thorny devil prompts reflection on the intricacies of nature's design.

Australia's northwest coast is home to the elusive dugong, often referred to as the "sea cow." These marine mammals, closely related to manatees, graze on seagrasses in shallow coastal waters. Spotting a dugong in its natural habitat offers a rare glimpse into the marine ecosystems that contribute to Australia's biodiversity.

Beyond the charismatic megafauna, Australia's insect world is equally fascinating. The iridescent jewel beetles, with their dazzling colors, and the industrious leafcutter ants, marching in disciplined lines, showcase the incredible diversity of invertebrate life. Exploring the intricate ecosystems supporting these tiny inhabitants adds a layer of appreciation for the interconnected web of life.

In summary, a wildlife encounter in Australia is a multifaceted journey through diverse ecosystems, each unveiling a chapter of the country's natural history. Whether it's a close encounter with iconic species or an exploration of the lesser-known inhabitants, the richness of Australia's wildlife offers a tapestry of experiences for those willing to venture into its wild landscapes.

4.2 Outdoor adventures

Begin your adventure in the heart of the country, exploring the iconic Uluru-Kata Tjuta National Park. As the sun paints the colossal red rock formations with warm hues, embark on a mesmerizing sunrise trek around Uluru. The spiritual significance of this sacred site adds a profound dimension to the experience, making it more than just a physical journey.

For water enthusiasts, the Great Barrier Reef is a must-visit destination. Dive into the crystal-clear waters teeming with vibrant coral reefs and exotic marine life. Snorkeling or scuba diving here is like entering a living kaleidoscope, where every twist and turn reveals a new world beneath the surface. The diversity of species and the sheer scale of the reef make it a bucket-list destination for any adventure seeker.

Head south to Tasmania, a rugged island state known for its untamed wilderness. Explore the famous Overland Track in Cradle Mountain-Lake St Clair National Park, a challenging trek that takes you through ancient rainforests, alpine meadows, and past glacial lakes. The changing landscapes provide a sensory feast, and the crisp mountain air invigorates the soul.

For those craving a more adrenaline-fueled experience, the Blue Mountains near Sydney offer world-class rock climbing opportunities. The towering sandstone cliffs and dramatic landscapes provide a thrilling backdrop as you ascend challenging routes. Abseiling down waterfalls adds an extra dose of excitement, combining technical skill with the beauty of cascading water.

Continue your journey to the Kimberley region in Western Australia, where the rugged terrain meets the Indian Ocean. Here, the Bungle Bungle Range in Purnululu National Park beckons with its unique beehive-shaped domes. Explore this ancient landscape on a helicopter tour for a bird's-eye view that showcases the grandeur of nature's architecture.

Venture into the Australian Alps during the winter months for a different kind of adventure. The snowy peaks offer excellent conditions for skiing and snowboarding, with resorts like Thredbo and Perisher providing a winter wonderland for snow enthusiasts. The crisp mountain air, powder-covered slopes, and panoramic views create a magical setting for snow sports.

For a coastal adventure, explore the pristine beaches of Queensland's Fraser Island. As the largest sand island in the world, Fraser Island boasts a unique ecosystem of rainforests growing on dunes. Navigate the island's sandy tracks in a 4WD vehicle, stopping at freshwater lakes, like the renowned Lake McKenzie, for a refreshing swim in crystal-clear waters.

Australia's vast and varied landscapes offer opportunities for adventure on land, in the water, and even beneath the surface. Whether you seek the thrill of scaling cliffs, diving into vibrant coral reefs, or trekking through ancient rainforests, the Land Down Under is a playground for outdoor enthusiasts, promising unforgettable experiences that connect you with the raw beauty of nature.

Chapter5.Cultural experiences

5.1 Food and Drink

Australian cuisine is heavily influenced by its indigenous roots. Bush tucker, comprising native ingredients like kangaroo, emu, bush tomatoes, and wattleseed, connects modern Australia to its ancient heritage. Indigenous cooking techniques, such as pit baking and using native plants for flavoring, continue to inspire contemporary chefs.

Moving beyond indigenous cuisine, Australia's multicultural society has shaped a vibrant food scene. Italian, Greek, Chinese, and Lebanese influences are prominent, contributing to a rich tapestry of flavors. Melbourne, often dubbed the "food capital," exemplifies this diversity with its myriad of international eateries and thriving coffee culture.

One cannot discuss Australian cuisine without mentioning the beloved meat pie. A staple at sporting events and gatherings, the meat pie is a pastry filled with minced meat, often beef, in a savory gravy. Another iconic dish is Vegemite, a yeast extract spread, enjoyed on toast or in sandwiches – an acquired taste that divides locals and intrigues visitors.

Seafood plays a significant role due to Australia's extensive coastline. Barramundi, mud crab, and Moreton Bay bugs are popular choices. The barbie (barbecue) is a quintessential Aussie experience, with prawns and snags (sausages) sizzling away at gatherings. The barbecue is a social institution, symbolizing outdoor living and camaraderie.

Australian wines have gained international acclaim, particularly those from regions like the Barossa Valley and Margaret River. Shiraz, Chardonnay, and Riesling are among the varietals that thrive in the diverse climates across the continent. The wine regions also offer picturesque landscapes, making wine tourism a growing industry.

In the realm of beverages, coffee holds a special place. Australians are discerning coffee drinkers, and the flat white, a combination of espresso and steamed milk with a thin layer of microfoam, is a local favorite. Cafés are integral to Australian culture, serving as meeting places and social hubs.

Craft beer has experienced a renaissance, with microbreweries popping up across the country. From hoppy IPAs to rich stouts, the craft beer scene caters to varied tastes. Traditional beer culture also thrives, with iconic brands like Victoria Bitter and XXXX maintaining their popularity.

Australia's commitment to sustainable and locally sourced produce is evident in its farmers' markets. These vibrant markets offer a cornucopia of fresh fruits, vegetables, cheeses, and artisanal products. The emphasis on farm-to-table dining has permeated the culinary scene, fostering a connection between producers and consumers.

Indigenous bush foods are making a resurgence, finding their way into contemporary dishes. Chefs are exploring the unique flavors of ingredients like quandong, Kakadu plum, and macadamia nuts, contributing to a renewed appreciation for native Australian ingredients.

In recent years, fusion cuisine has gained momentum, blending traditional Australian elements with global influences. This culinary experimentation is visible in modern Australian fine dining, where chefs push boundaries and create innovative dishes that reflect the country's evolving gastronomic identity.

In conclusion, Australia's food and drink scene is a delightful mosaic, reflecting a harmonious blend of indigenous traditions, multicultural influences, and a commitment to innovation. Whether savoring a meat pie at a local bakery, enjoying a flat white in a Melbourne laneway café, or exploring the diverse offerings at a farmers' market, the culinary journey in Australia is a celebration of flavor, diversity, and a deep connection to the land.

5.2 Australian cuisine

From the sun-kissed shores to the vast outback, Australia's food culture has evolved, incorporating flavors from Europe, Asia, and the Middle East. Let's delve into the rich and varied landscape of Australian cuisine.

Indigenous Influences

At the heart of Australian cuisine lies the traditional food of the Aboriginal people, the country's original inhabitants. Bush tucker, as it's commonly known, includes native ingredients like kangaroo, emu, bush tomatoes, and quandong. Indigenous Australians have a deep connection to the land, using unique cooking methods such as baking in the ground with hot coals and creating earth ovens.

Barbecue Culture

Aussies are renowned for their love of barbecues, or "barbies" as they affectionately call them. Grilling is not just a cooking method; it's a way of life. Whether it's a beachside gathering or a backyard party, barbecues often feature classic Australian fare like sausages, lamb chops, and seafood. The smoky aroma of a sizzling barbecue is an integral part of the Australian culinary experience.

Seafood Sensation

Given its extensive coastline, seafood plays a prominent role in Australian cuisine. From succulent prawns to Moreton Bay bugs and Tasmanian salmon, the variety is staggering. Fish and chips, a beloved takeaway dish, showcase Australia's affinity for fresh, locally sourced seafood. Sydney's famous Sydney Rock Oysters and Queensland's mud crabs are culinary delights that seafood enthusiasts can't resist.

Multicultural Mosaic

Australia's multicultural society has brought a plethora of flavors to the table. Italian, Greek, Chinese, and Lebanese cuisines have seamlessly integrated into the Australian culinary landscape. Melbourne, in particular, is a melting pot of diverse food cultures, boasting an array of international restaurants and food markets. Dim sum, pasta, souvlaki, and kebabs are just a few examples of the multicultural tapestry woven into the Australian dining experience.

Meat Pies and Sausage Rolls

Considered iconic Aussie snack meat pies and sausage rolls are ubiquitous. Whether enjoyed at a sports game or as a quick lunch, these savory pastries are filled with minced meat, often beef, and encased in flaky pastry. They are commonly accompanied by tomato sauce (ketchup), and the combination is a nostalgic comfort food for many Australians.

Avocado Smash and Flat Whites

Australia has made a mark on the global brunch scene with its popular dish, avocado smash. Mashed avocado on sourdough toast, adorned with toppings like poached eggs, feta, and cherry tomatoes, epitomizes the vibrant and health-conscious modern Australian dining culture. Accompanying this brunch delight is the flat white, a velvety espresso-based coffee with steamed milk, showcasing Australia's serious coffee culture.

Bush Herbs and Spices

The Australian landscape contributes unique herbs and spices to the culinary palette. Wattleseed, bush tomato, and lemon myrtle are among the indigenous ingredients that impart distinct flavors to dishes. These ingredients are not only used in traditional Aboriginal cuisine but have also found their way into modern Australian cooking, adding a touch of local authenticity.

Desserts Down Under

Australian desserts are a sweet celebration of flavors. Pavlova, a meringue-based dessert named after the Russian ballerina Anna Pavlova, is a national favorite. Tim Tams, chocolate-coated biscuits, have a cult following, and lamingtons, sponge cake squares coated in chocolate icing and desiccated coconut, are staples in afternoon teas.

Australian Wine and Beer

Australia is renowned for its world-class wines, particularly Shiraz and Chardonnay. The wine regions of Barossa Valley, Margaret River, and Hunter Valley produce exceptional vintages. In addition to wine, beer holds a special place in Australian culture. Local brews like Victoria Bitter (VB) and XXXX are enjoyed at pubs and social gatherings across the country.

In conclusion, Australian cuisine is a dynamic fusion of indigenous traditions, global influences, and a deep appreciation for fresh, high-quality ingredients. From the sizzle of the barbecue to the delicate flavors of native herbs, Australia's food scene reflects the nation's diverse cultural tapestry and its love affair with good food and company.

5.3 Dining etiquette

Dining etiquette in Australia is characterized by a casual yet respectful atmosphere. Australians generally value a relaxed and informal dining experience, but certain etiquette norms still apply. Understanding these customs can enhance your dining experience and help you navigate social situations with ease.

1. Reservations

In more formal dining establishments, it's advisable to make reservations, especially during peak hours. This shows consideration for the restaurant's capacity and helps ensure a smoother experience.

2. Punctuality

Australians appreciate punctuality. Arriving on time for a reservation or when invited to someone's home is a sign of respect. If you're running late, it's courteous to inform the host or restaurant.

3. Table Manners

Basic table manners are expected. Chew with your mouth closed, and avoid talking with your mouth full. Keep elbows off the table, and use utensils appropriately. If unsure, observe the locals around you.

4. Tipping

Tipping is generally not as prevalent in Australia as in some other countries. However, it is appreciated for exceptional service. Ten percent is customary in restaurants, but tipping is not mandatory.

5. BYO (Bring Your Own)

Some restaurants in Australia allow patrons to bring their wine. However, this is usually subject to a corkage fee. Check the restaurant's policy beforehand, and if bringing your own, choose a wine that complements the cuisine.

6. Ordering

When ordering food, be aware of any dietary restrictions or preferences. Australians are generally accommodating, but it's courteous to inform the waiter of any specific requirements. It's also customary to wait until everyone at the table has received their food before starting to eat.

7. Engaging in Conversation

Australians are friendly and enjoy casual conversation. Feel free to engage in small talk, but avoid controversial topics like politics and religion, especially with people you've just met.

8. Wine Culture

Australia is known for its wine, and it's common for Australians to enjoy wine with their meals. If you're offered a glass, it's polite to accept, even if you choose not to drink alcohol.

9. Thanking the Chef

If you've enjoyed your meal, it's a nice touch to pass on your compliments to the chef or kitchen staff. This gesture is appreciated and reinforces positive feedback.

10. Paying the Bill

When dining with others, it's common to split the bill evenly, especially in casual settings. In more formal situations, the person who extended the invitation may offer to pay, but it's considerate to offer to contribute.

11. Dress Code

Australia generally has a relaxed approach to dress codes, but it's wise to check if the restaurant has any specific requirements. Casual attire is often acceptable in many places.

12. Leftovers

Taking leftovers home from a restaurant is becoming more acceptable, but it's always good to ask the staff if it's okay. In many cases, staff will offer to pack the leftovers for you.

In conclusion, while Australians appreciate a laid-back atmosphere, observing basic etiquette enhances the dining experience for everyone involved. Being respectful, punctual, and considerate of others' preferences will help you navigate the diverse culinary landscape of Australia with ease.

Chapter 6.Health and Safety

6.1 Vaccinations and Health Precautions

Vaccination and health precautions in Australia play a crucial role in safeguarding public health and preventing the spread of infectious diseases. The country has a robust immunization program supported by rigorous regulatory frameworks and public health initiatives.

Vaccination Programs

Australia has a comprehensive national immunization program that provides vaccines to eligible individuals at no cost. This program aims to protect Australians against vaccine-preventable diseases such as measles, mumps, rubella, influenza, and more. Vaccinations are administered through various channels, including general practitioners, vaccination clinics, and school-based programs.

Childhood Immunization

Childhood vaccination is a cornerstone of public health in Australia. The National Immunisation Program Schedule outlines the recommended vaccines for infants and young children. These vaccines, including those for diphtheria, tetanus, pertussis, hepatitis B, and others, are essential for building immunity early in life.

Influenza Vaccination

Annual influenza vaccination is strongly recommended for individuals of all ages, especially those at higher risk of complications, such as the elderly, pregnant women, and individuals with chronic health conditions. The influenza vaccine helps reduce the severity and spread of seasonal flu.

COVID-19 Vaccination

The COVID-19 vaccination campaign in Australia has been a critical response to the global pandemic. The government has rolled out vaccination programs to ensure widespread access to vaccines, with priority given to high-risk groups. Regular updates and communication from health authorities keep the public informed about vaccine safety and efficacy.

Travel Vaccinations

Australia, being a popular destination, emphasizes travel vaccinations to prevent the importation and spread of infectious diseases. Travelers are advised to check their immunization status and get relevant vaccines before departing, depending on the destination and potential health risks.

Health Precautions

Beyond vaccinations, Australia promotes various health precautions to maintain overall well-being. These include

Hygiene Practices: Encouraging regular handwashing and the use of hand sanitizers helps prevent the spread of infections.

Food Safety: Following proper food handling and hygiene practices reduces the risk of foodborne illnesses.

Vector-borne Diseases: In some regions, precautions against diseases transmitted by mosquitoes, ticks, and other vectors are essential. This includes using insect repellent and protective clothing.

Sun Protection: Given Australia's high UV index, sun protection is crucial. This involves using sunscreen, wearing protective clothing, and seeking shade during peak sunlight hours.

Mental Health Support: Recognizing the importance of mental health, Australia emphasizes resources and support for mental well-being. Accessible mental health services help individuals cope with stressors and challenges.

Public Health Campaigns:
Public health campaigns in Australia are instrumental in promoting vaccination and health precautions. These campaigns leverage various media channels to disseminate information, debunk myths, and encourage participation in vaccination programs.

Regulatory Framework
Australia's Therapeutic Goods Administration (TGA) is responsible for regulating vaccines and ensuring their safety and efficacy. Rigorous testing and monitoring processes are in place to

maintain the highest standards for vaccines available in the country.

In conclusion, Australia's vaccination and health precautions form a comprehensive strategy to protect public health. Through robust vaccination programs, targeted health precautions, and public awareness campaigns, the country strives to create a resilient and healthy population. These efforts not only prevent the spread of infectious diseases but also contribute to the overall well-being of individuals and communities across the nation.

6.2 Emergency services

Emergency services in Australia play a crucial role in ensuring the safety and well-being of the population. Comprising various agencies and organizations, these services are designed to respond promptly to a wide range of emergencies, from natural disasters to medical emergencies and other incidents that pose a threat to public safety. This comprehensive network of emergency responders and support systems reflects Australia's commitment to protecting its citizens and minimizing the impact of unforeseen events.

One of the key components of Australia's emergency services is the firefighting sector. Given the country's diverse landscapes, which include dense forests and bush areas, wildfires are a significant threat. The Rural Fire Service (RFS) is a vital organization that operates at the forefront of firefighting efforts, particularly in rural and regional areas. This volunteer-based service is equipped with specialized training and resources to combat bushfires, protect communities, and coordinate evacuation efforts when necessary.

In addition to wildfires, urban areas face the risk of structure fires, requiring the intervention of metropolitan fire services.

These services are typically comprised of professional firefighters who respond to emergencies in densely populated areas. Their responsibilities include not only extinguishing fires but also rescuing individuals from hazardous situations, providing emergency medical assistance, and educating the public on fire safety.

Australia's emergency medical services (EMS) are another critical component of the emergency response system. Ambulance services operate across the country, responding to medical emergencies ranging from accidents and injuries to heart attacks and other life-threatening conditions. These services are staffed by highly trained paramedics who deliver pre-hospital care, stabilize patients, and transport them to medical facilities for further treatment.

The State Emergency Service (SES) is a versatile organization that plays a crucial role in responding to a variety of emergencies. This includes flood and storm responses, where SES volunteers work to ensure the safety of communities affected by adverse weather conditions. They may be involved in tasks such as sandbagging, road closures, and rescues from floodwaters. The SES also assists in search and rescue operations, responding to incidents where individuals are lost or trapped in challenging environments.

Law enforcement agencies are integral to emergency response efforts as well. Police services operate at the local, state, and federal levels, maintaining public order and safety. In times of crisis, they collaborate with other emergency services to manage incidents, control crowds, and enforce evacuation orders when necessary. The Australian Federal Police (AFP) also plays a role in national security and responds to incidents that extend beyond state borders.

Australia's emergency management framework emphasizes coordination and collaboration among various agencies. The Australian Government, through agencies like Emergency Management Australia (EMA), provides support and coordination at the national level. EMA works closely with state and territory emergency management agencies to enhance preparedness, response, recovery, and mitigation efforts across the country.

The coordination of emergency services is facilitated through the use of advanced technology and communication systems. Emergency warning systems, such as text messages, sirens, and social media alerts, are employed to notify the public of imminent threats and provide guidance on protective actions. This ensures that individuals are well-informed and can take appropriate measures to safeguard themselves and their communities.

Training and preparedness are ongoing priorities for emergency services in Australia. Regular drills and exercises are conducted to simulate various emergency scenarios, allowing responders to practice their skills and evaluate the effectiveness of their strategies. This continuous training enhances the overall capability of emergency services to respond swiftly and efficiently to real-life incidents.

Community engagement is a crucial aspect of emergency management in Australia. Public education programs aim to raise awareness about potential hazards, encourage preparedness, and educate individuals on how to respond during emergencies. This collaborative approach fosters a sense of shared responsibility and resilience within communities, empowering individuals to take proactive measures to protect themselves and their neighbors.

Australia's emergency services operate as a comprehensive and integrated system, encompassing firefighting, medical response, search and rescue, law enforcement, and emergency management. This multifaceted approach reflects the diverse range of threats and challenges faced by the country, from natural disasters to urban emergencies. Through effective coordination, advanced technology, ongoing training, and community engagement, Australia's emergency services play a vital role in safeguarding lives and minimizing the impact of emergencies on the nation as a whole.

Chapter 7.Safety Tips

7.1 Packing Tips

Packing for a trip to Australia requires thoughtful consideration due to the country's diverse climates, ranging from tropical in the north to temperate in the south. Here's a comprehensive guide with tips to ensure you're well-prepared for your Australian adventure.

Clothing

Layering is Key

Australia's weather can be unpredictable. Pack lightweight layers that you can easily add or remove.
Include a mix of short and long-sleeved shirts, a sweater, and a waterproof jacket.
Swimwear:

Don't forget your swimsuit! Australia boasts stunning beaches, and you might find yourself near water at some point.

Comfortable Shoes

Whether exploring cities or hiking national parks, comfortable shoes are a must. Include a pair suitable for walking and possibly hiking.

Hat and Sunglasses

Protect yourself from the strong Australian sun with a wide-brimmed hat and sunglasses.

Essentials

Power Adapter

Australia uses Type I electrical outlets, so ensure you have the right adapter for your devices.
Sunscreen:

UV rays are intense in Australia. Pack a high-SPF sunscreen to protect your skin.

Insect Repellent

Especially important if you're venturing into tropical areas where insects are more prevalent.

Reusable Water Bottle

Stay hydrated, especially in warmer regions. A reusable bottle is eco-friendly and practical.

Health and Safety

First Aid Kit

Include basic medications, bandages, and any prescription medicines you might need.

Travel Insurance

Ensure you have comprehensive travel insurance covering medical emergencies.

Electronics

Camera

Australia's landscapes are breathtaking. Bring a good camera to capture memories. Portable Charger:

Keep your devices charged, especially if you're spending time outdoors.

Documentation

Passport and Visa

Check your passport's validity and ensure you have the necessary visas.

Emergency Information

Carry a list of emergency contacts, including local services and the nearest embassy.

Money and Banking

Currency

Australian dollars are the local currency. Inform your bank of your travel dates to avoid any issues with your cards.

Travel Wallet

Keep your money, cards, and important documents organized in a secure travel wallet.

Backpack

Daypack
A small backpack for day trips is handy. Pack essentials like water, snacks, and a map.

Specific Activities

Snorkeling Gear

If you plan to explore the Great Barrier Reef or other marine areas, consider bringing your snorkeling gear.

Camping Gear

If camping is on your itinerary, pack a lightweight tent, sleeping bag, and other camping essentials.

Cultural Considerations

Modest Clothing

Respect local customs, especially in more conservative areas. Pack modest clothing.

Reusable Bag

Australia is environmentally conscious. Carry a reusable bag for shopping.

Miscellaneous

Language Translation App

While English is the primary language, having a translation app can be helpful in certain situations.

Travel Pillow

Make long journeys more comfortable with a compact travel pillow.

Final Tips

Check Weather Forecast

Australia's weather can vary significantly. Check forecasts for specific regions during your stay.

Pack Smart

Be mindful of baggage limits, especially if you plan on taking domestic flights within Australia.

Local SIM Card

Consider getting a local SIM card for your phone to avoid high roaming charges.

By keeping these tips in mind, you'll be well-equipped for an amazing journey through Australia's diverse landscapes and vibrant cities. Safe travels!

Conclusion

Australia, a vast and diverse continent, beckons travelers with its unique blend of natural wonders, vibrant cities, and rich cultural experiences. As we conclude this comprehensive travel guide, it's evident that Australia offers a myriad of attractions that cater to every type of adventurer.

Commencing our journey in the iconic city of Sydney, visitors are greeted by the world-famous Sydney Opera House and the Sydney Harbour Bridge. These architectural marvels stand as testaments to Australia's modernity and innovation. Exploring the bustling streets of Sydney unveils a dynamic cultural scene, with art galleries, museums, and a thriving culinary landscape that showcases the nation's multicultural influences.

Venturing beyond the urban landscape, Australia's natural beauty takes center stage. The Great Barrier Reef, a UNESCO World Heritage site, is a kaleidoscope of marine life that captivates divers and snorkelers alike. Our guide emphasizes the importance of responsible tourism to preserve this delicate ecosystem for future generations.

Embarking on an outback adventure reveals the rugged heart of Australia. The vast expanses of red desert, punctuated by ancient rock formations like Uluru, provide a spiritual connection to the land. Travelers are encouraged to engage with Indigenous communities, respecting their traditions and gaining insights into the world's oldest living culture.

Moving south to Melbourne, we discover a city renowned for its arts and coffee culture. Laneways adorned with street art lead to hidden cafes and boutiques, offering a unique blend of creativity and innovation. The nearby Great Ocean Road presents a scenic drive along dramatic cliffs and pristine beaches, showcasing the raw beauty of Australia's coastline.

Nature enthusiasts will find solace in the lush landscapes of Tasmania, an island state brimming with national parks and wilderness areas. Cradle Mountain and Freycinet National Park are among the highlights, providing hiking trails that immerse visitors in untouched wilderness.

Our guide underlines the significance of Australia's wildlife, emphasizing encounters with unique creatures like kangaroos, koalas, and the elusive platypus. Conservation efforts are spotlighted, encouraging travelers to contribute to the protection of Australia's diverse fauna.

In the tropical north, Cairns serves as a gateway to the ancient Daintree Rainforest and the captivating Kuranda Scenic Railway. The juxtaposition of dense foliage and vibrant wildlife against the backdrop of the Coral Sea creates an enchanting experience for those seeking immersion in nature.

As we conclude our exploration, it's essential to address the vast distances in Australia. The guide emphasizes efficient travel planning, utilizing domestic flights and well-established road networks to optimize time and cover the expansive terrain.

In conclusion, Australia stands as a multifaceted destination that caters to the intrepid explorer, culture enthusiast, and nature lover alike. This travel guide aims to empower visitors with the knowledge to appreciate Australia's diverse offerings while promoting responsible tourism practices. Whether marveling at urban landmarks, diving into the depths of the Great Barrier Reef, or traversing the rugged outback, every corner of Australia tells a unique story waiting to be explored. Safe travels!

Final Thought

Embarking on a journey to the land down under, Australia is a venture into a realm of diverse landscapes, unique wildlife, and vibrant cultures. As the curtains close on my Australian escapade, a flood of memories and impressions rushes in, creating a mosaic of experiences that define this chapter in my travelogue.

The journey began with the iconic Sydney Opera House standing proudly against the azure backdrop of the harbor. Its distinctive architecture echoed the modern spirit of the city, a blend of innovation and artistic finesse. The Sydney Harbour Bridge, an engineering marvel, provided a thrilling ascent, offering panoramic views that stretched from the city skyline to the distant horizons.

Venturing into the heart of the continent led me to the mystical Uluru, a colossal monolith steeped in Aboriginal significance. The changing hues of Uluru at sunrise and sunset painted a canvas of ethereal beauty, leaving an indelible mark on my soul. It was a humbling experience to learn about the cultural importance of this sacred site and to witness the profound connection the Anangu people have with their ancestral lands.

The Great Barrier Reef beckoned, unveiling a kaleidoscope of underwater wonders. Snorkeling through vibrant coral gardens, I was immersed in a world teeming with marine life. The delicate balance of this ecosystem and the urgent need for conservation became apparent, prompting reflection on our collective responsibility to protect such natural treasures.

Australia's cities, like Melbourne, offer a contrasting urban vibe. The labyrinthine laneways, adorned with street art, breathed life into the city's creative spirit. Exploring the Melbourne Cricket Ground, an iconic sports arena, provided a glimpse into Australia's fervent passion for cricket, an integral part of its cultural fabric.

A road trip along the Great Ocean Road was a cinematic journey along rugged cliffs and pristine beaches. The Twelve Apostles, standing resilient against the relentless ocean, showcased nature's unwavering power and the transience of geological formations. Each stop along the coastal drive unveiled a new facet of Australia's untamed beauty.

Encounters with unique wildlife were a highlight of the trip. From cuddly koalas to bounding kangaroos, Australia's fauna exhibited a charm that transcended postcard clichés. The sprawling landscapes of Kangaroo Island offered a sanctuary for diverse species, a testament to Australia's commitment to wildlife conservation.

Indigenous experiences provided a profound insight into Australia's rich cultural tapestry. The didgeridoo's haunting melody echoed through the air during an Aboriginal performance, underscoring the enduring legacy of the world's oldest living culture. Engaging with Aboriginal art and storytelling reinforced the importance of preserving and respecting indigenous heritage.

Culinary adventures unfolded as I savored the diverse flavors of Australian cuisine. From fresh seafood in Sydney's bustling markets to savoring a traditional Aussie barbecue in the outback, each meal was a gastronomic journey reflecting the country's culinary diversity. The fusion of global influences and locally sourced ingredients created a unique palate that mirrored Australia's multicultural identity.

As I reflect on my Australian odyssey, the vastness of the Outback, the allure of coastal wonders, and the urban dynamism of its cities converge into a mosaic of experiences. Australia, with its unique blend of natural wonders and cultural richness, has left an indelible imprint on my travel narrative. It is a country where ancient landscapes harmonize with modern urbanity, creating a tapestry that captivates the senses and sparks a desire to delve deeper into its multifaceted allure.

Printed in Great Britain
by Amazon

38011378R00066